GRAMMAR

PUPIL BOOK A

WENDY WREN

Nelson

Book A – Contents

This symbol shows that you
need to correct mistakes in
the text.

The alphabet

These letters make up our **alphabet**.
These are small letters:

a b c d e f g h i j k l m

n o p q r s t u v w x y z

These are capital letters:

A B C D E F G H I J K L M

N O P Q R S T U V W X Y Z

GRAMMAR *Focus*

These are small letters.

Answer these questions about the **alphabet**.
Write the letters in your book.

1 What letter comes before **w**?

2 What letter comes after **g**?

3 What is the first letter of the alphabet?

4 What is the last letter of the alphabet?

5 What letter comes before **m**?

A Copy these **alphabets**.
Fill in the missing letters.

1. a b c _ e f g _ i j k _ m
n o _ q r s _ u v w _ y z

2. a _ c d _ f g _ i j _ l m
_ o p _ r s _ u v _ x y _

3. _ _ C D E _ _ H I J _ _ M N
_ _ Q R _ _ U V _ _ Y Z

B These words have mixed capital letters and small letters.
Write the words using only **small letters**.

Use the alphabet on page 4 to help you.

1 wEt

2 hiLL

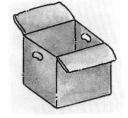

3 boX

4 sOck

5 DUCk

6 juG

5

Naming words

The words below are **naming words**.
They tell us the names of things.

| Naming words are called nouns. |

tap   fan   rat

GRAMMAR *Focus*

Add a letter to complete each of these
naming words. Write the words in your book.

1 ca_   2 v_n   3 _en   4 _an

5 je_   6 b_d   7 _in   8 he_

Look at this picture.

Be careful!
Some of these
naming words
are not in the
picture.

Copy the **naming words** below.
Tick the words you can see in the picture.

1 log	2 cat	3 van	4 fox
5 pin	6 sun	7 fan	8 hut
9 tap	10 jet	11 mop	12 man

Describing words

The words below are **describing words**.
They tell us more about a person or a thing.

Describing words
are called
adjectives.

a **red** pen   a **hot** drink   a **bent** pin

GRAMMAR *Focus*

Add a letter to complete each of
these **describing words**.
Write the words in your book.

1 a fa_ cat   2 a _ig sack   3 a sa_ boy

4 a gr_en hat   5 a _et day   6 a dee_ well

Look at this picture.

Think of what each thing looks like.

Choose a **describing word** from the box for these things in the picture.

1 a _____ cake

2 a _____ hat

3 a _____ balloon

4 a _____ jelly

5 a _____ present

red   paper

green

birthday

big

Naming words and describing words

A describing word tells us about a naming word.

The words below are **naming words**.
They tell us the names of things.

a **tent**   a **man**

The words below are **describing words**.
They tell us more about a person or thing.

a **red** tent   an **old** man

GRAMMAR *Focus*

Match a **naming word** with a **describing word** for each picture.
Write the pairs of words in your book.

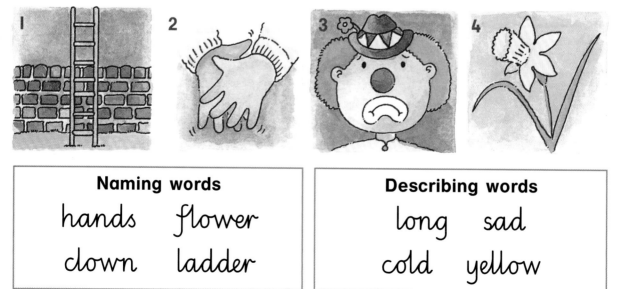

Naming words	
hands	flower
clown	ladder

Describing words	
long	sad
cold	yellow

A naming word tells us the name of something.

A Copy the **naming words** from these sentences.

1 This is a green bag.

2 Can you see the big bird?

3 Where is the little duck?

4 Get a warm hat.

5 He is a thin man.

B Copy the **describing words** from these sentences.

A describing word tells us more about a naming word.

1 The hot drink is ready.

2 This is a long road.

3 The black dog is lost.

4 This is a wet mop.

5 Can you see the large clouds?

11

Doing words

The words below are **doing words**.
They tell us what people are doing.

Doing words are
called verbs.

hopping   **hitting**   **cutting**

GRAMMAR *Focus*

What are these people doing?
Choose the correct **doing words** from the box.
Write the words in your book.

sucking
kicking
yelling
waving

1 _____   2 _____

3 _____   4 _____

Look at what
they are doing.

Use a **doing word** from the box to answer
each question.
The first one is done for you.

sleeping   winking   eating

reading   running   singing

I What is the girl
doing?

2 What is the boy
doing?

3 What is the
woman doing?

eating

4 What is the baby
doing?

5 What is the man
doing?

6 What is the dog
doing?

13

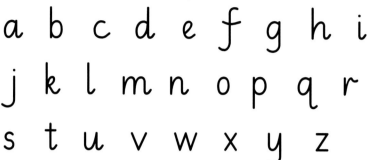
Alphabetical order

This is our **alphabet**.

a b c d e f g h i

j k l m n o p q r

s t u v w x y z

This is how we write small letters.

Words in a dictionary are in **alphabetical order**. Look at the first letters of these words.

apple   book   cat

The words are in alphabetical order.

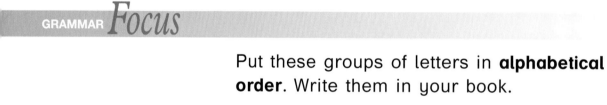
Put these groups of letters in **alphabetical order**. Write them in your book.

Use the alphabet at the top of the page to help you.

1 b   c   a

2 f   e   g

3 k   l   j

4 o   n   p

5 u   t   s

Write these words in **alphabetical order**.
Look at the first letter of each word.

1

bell   ant   can   dog

2

pin   nut   owl   mop

3

jelly   hat   ink   kick

4

umbrella   van   sack   tram

Doing words

The words below are **doing words**.
They tell us what people or animals
are doing.

Doing words are
called verbs.

driving   **digging**   **pecking**

What are these animals doing?
Choose a **doing word** from the box
for each picture.
Write the words in your book.

Look at what
the animals
are doing.

scratching
hopping
playing
growling

1 _____   2 _____

3 _____   4 _____

Think about what each animal can do. They can all do more than one thing!

What can each animal do?
Copy the right **doing words** from each box.

1

fly   roar
shout   sing

2

fly   swim   grow   climb

3

eat   bark   hunt   speak

4

jump   climb   sleep   whistle

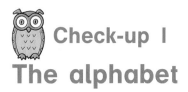

Check-up 1

The alphabet

Copy this **alphabet** into your book.
Fill in the missing letters.

_ _ c d _ f _ _ _ j _ l m
n _ _ q _ s _ _ v w _ y _

Alphabetical order

Put each of these groups of words into **alphabetical order**.

1	sell queen rock trick
2	log jump kick men
3	owl mop pen not
4	van well ten up

Naming words

Copy the **naming words** from each list.

1	is pin sock bus
2	jug cup his at
3	not pen bed bat
4	bad man an leg
5	fed wet peg hill

Describing words

Copy the **describing words** from each list.

1 | peg   red   tidy   bed
2 | old   cot   sad   long
3 | pet   ten   green   fog
4 | hot   dog   box   cold
5 | thin   mug   happy   bun

Doing words

A What are these people **doing**?

1 _____   2 _____   3 _____   4 _____

B Copy the **doing word** from each sentence.

1 The seal swims in the sea.

2 The fox drinks the water.

3 The snake hisses at the man.

4 The mouse nibbles the cheese.

5 The spider spins the web.

More than one

We add **s** to lots of words when we mean **more than one**.

Singular means 'one'. **Plural** means 'more than one'.

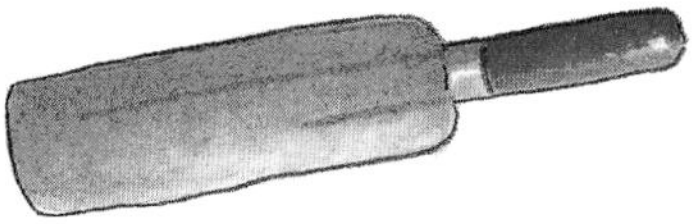

one bat

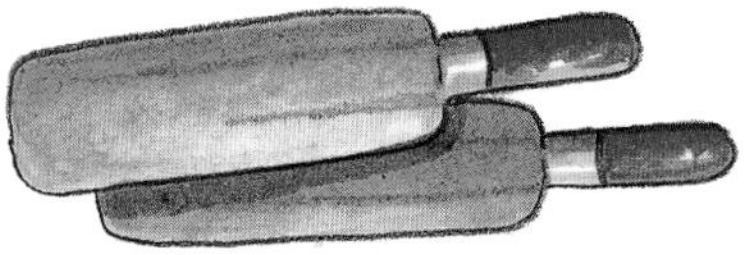

two bat**s**

one ball

five ball**s**

What are the missing words that go with these pictures? Write them in your book.

1 one hill   two ____

2 one cup   three ____

3 one duck   four ____

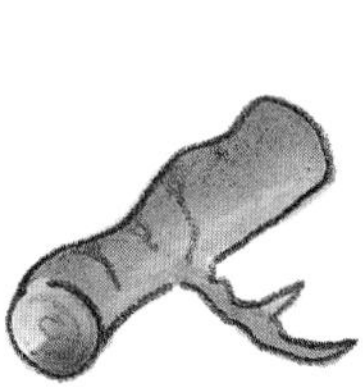

4 one log   five ____

A Write what you can see in each picture.

1 two _____	2 five _____	3 three _____

B Look at the words below.
Copy the words that mean **more than one**.

legs   pet

bat   hands

tents   rocks

jug   bells

hill   bulls

Special naming words

Names of people are **special naming words**. Special naming words begin with capital letters.

Gary

Laura

The names you give your pets are **special naming words**.

Tigger   Snowy

GRAMMAR *Focus*

Remember!
Special naming
words begin with
capital letters.

Find the **special naming words** in each sentence.
Write them in your book.

1 Raju likes to play football.

2 Chris and Lara are friends.

3 Is your name Jack?

4 Our dog is called Poppy.

Practice

Remember the capital letters.

A What names would you give these pets? Think of a **special naming word** for each pet.

1 _____

2 _____

3 _____

4 _____

5 _____

6 _____

B In your book, write:

1 your name

2 the name of your friend

3 the name of your teacher

4 the name you would like to be called

23

Writing sentences

A **sentence** starts with a **capital letter**.
A sentence usually ends with a **full stop**.
These are sentences:

Sentences must make sense.

The bell is ringing**.**   **T**his sack is torn**.**

GRAMMAR *Focus*

A Here is the alphabet in small letters.

a b c d e f g h i j k l m
n o p q r s t u v w x y z

In your book, write the alphabet in **capital letters**.

B Copy these **sentences**.
Put in the missing **capital letters** and **full stops**.

1 sita has hurt her leg

2 we are going fishing today

3 the boys got on the bus

4 tom wrote a letter to his friend

Look for the
capital letters
and full stops.

Make **sentences** by putting the words in the
right order.
The pictures will help you.

1 are a The snowman.
children making

2 playing park. The in
twins are the

3 will My start.
car not

4 read book. have
I this

25

Doing words

The blue words below are **doing words**.

Doing words are called verbs.

The boy **throws** the stick.

The dog **fetches** the stick.

GRAMMAR *Focus*

Write the **doing words** in your book.

1 The bull chases the man.

2 The girl bangs the door.

3 The monkey climbs the tree.

Write a sentence to show what is being done in each picture.

1

2

3

4

Describing words

Describing words tell us more about a person or thing.

Describing words are called adjectives.

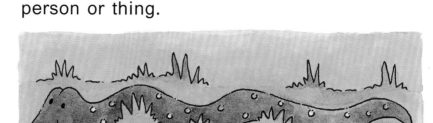

The **long** snake is hiding in the **green** grass.

GRAMMAR *Focus*

Write the **describing words** in your book.

Number 3 has two describing words.

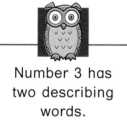

1 The red flag is flying today.

2 The small boy is crying.

3 The dirty coat and muddy boots are on the floor.

Copy the sentences below.
Add **describing words** of your own to finish them.

Describing words make sentences more interesting.

1 The _____ sun is setting over the _____ sea.

2 The _____ giraffe is eating the _____ leaves.

3 The _____ clouds are covering the _____ moon.

4 The _____ rabbit is hiding behind the _____ tree.

Writing sentences

A **sentence** starts with a **capital letter** and usually ends with a **full stop**.

Sentences must make sense.

Tracy is waiting for the bus**.**

It is raining**.**

She is very wet**.**

GRAMMAR *Focus*

Copy these **sentences** into your book.
Put rings around the **capital letters** and **full stops**.

1 The duck is swimming on the pond.

2 Simon looked at the clock.

3 My pen has run out of ink.

4 Please post this letter for me.

5 The tin is on the top shelf.

GRAMMAR *Practice*

Look at the pictures.
Write a **sentence** about each picture.

More than one

Look at the words below.
Copy the words that mean **more than one**.

rings	cots	click
snails	king	bells
mill	cups	neck
locks	hats	door

Special naming words

Copy the **special naming word** from each sentence.

1 The twins are called Alice and Alan.

2 My pet snake is called Sam.

3 Sara likes to swim.

4 Beauty is a black horse.

Writing sentences

A Copy these **sentences**.
Put in the missing capital letters and full stops.

1 the house is very old

2 it has no door

3 some windows are broken

B Make **sentences** by putting the words in the right order

1 holes roof. are There the in

2 weeds. is The full garden of

3 old Rain house. into gets the

Doing words

Use these **doing words** in sentences of your own.

1 sing 2 jump

3 run 4 kick

5 peck 6 play

7 clap 8 eat

Describing words

Add a **describing word** to each sentence to make it more interesting.

1 The clock is in the hall.

2 I found this shell on the beach.

3 I can see the moon.

4 There are sheep in the field.

Questions

Some sentences **tell us something**.
Telling sentences end with a **full stop**.

It is windy today.

Try writing a few
question marks.

Some sentences **ask us something**.
Asking sentences end with a **question mark**.

Is it windy today?

Asking sentences are called **questions**.

GRAMMAR *Focus*

Look for the
question marks.

Copy the **questions** into your book.

1 Where are you going?

2 I am going to the shops.

3 What are you going to buy?

4 I am going to buy apples.

5 Will you get some oranges too?

6 We have oranges in the bowl.

A Copy these sentences.
End the telling sentences with a **full stop**.
End the asking sentences with a
question mark.

1 Do you like cheese

2 I like to drink milk

3 Will you stay for tea

4 Is it ready now

5 Can I help you

B Complete these **questions**.

1 Where are _____

2 Why does _____

3 When can _____

4 What is _____

5 Who will _____

35

Naming words

Naming words tell us the names of things.

tree   book   ship

Naming words
are called nouns.

GRAMMAR *Focus*

What are the **naming words** for these pictures?
Write the words in your book.

1 b _ _

 2 b _ _ _

3 n _ _ _

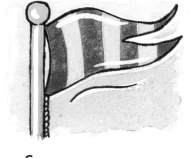

4 s _ _ _

5 f _ _ _

6 k _ _ _

Look at this picture.

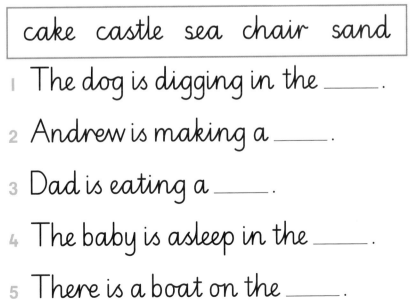

Copy the sentences below.
Complete them, using **naming words** from the box.

cake   castle   sea   chair   sand

1 The dog is digging in the ＿＿.

2 Andrew is making a ＿＿.

3 Dad is eating a ＿＿.

4 The baby is asleep in the ＿＿.

5 There is a boat on the ＿＿.

Doing words

Doing words tell us what people and animals are doing.

Doing words are called verbs.

The boy **feeds** the bird.

The bird **pecks** the ground.

Doing words also tell us what things are doing.

The wind **blows**.
The tree **bends**.
The leaves **fall**.

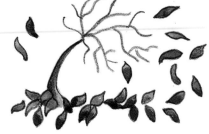

GRAMMAR *Focus*

What are these things doing?
Choose a **doing word** from the box for each picture.
Write the words in your book.

dripping	shining	falling	flying

1 _____ 2 _____ 3 _____ 4 _____

Look at the pictures below.
Use a **doing word** from the box to answer
each question.
The first one is done for you.

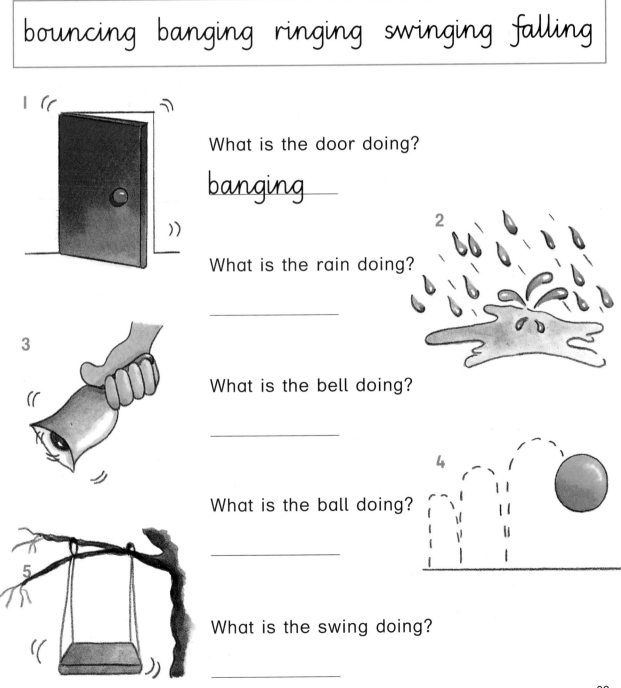

bouncing   banging   ringing   swinging   falling

1

What is the door doing?

banging

2

What is the rain doing?

_____

3

What is the bell doing?

_____

4

What is the ball doing?

_____

5

What is the swing doing?

_____

Special naming words

Special naming words are called proper nouns.

Special naming words begin with a capital letter.

Names of people are special naming words.

Names of pets are special naming words.

Mrs Brown has two cats.
They are called **Sandy** and **Mandy**.

GRAMMAR *Focus*

Find the **special naming words** in each sentence.
Write them in your book.

1 My pony is called Lucky.

2 Mr Clark and Mr Kasim are friends.

3 Sue has a hamster called Bunty.

4 We have called our stick insects Twig and Mig.

A Use **special naming words** to answer these questions.

    1 What is your first name?

    2 What is your last name?

    3 What is your middle name?

B Look at this picture.

Rose   Jessica   Sanjay   Rory

Remember the capital letters.

Use **special naming words** to answer each question.

    1 Who lives at number 3?

    2 Who lives at number 2?

    3 Who lives at number 1?

    4 Who lives at number 4?

    5 Who has a dog?

    6 Who has a cat?

Writing sentences

Sentences must make sense.

Telling sentences end with a full stop.

The car is stuck in the mud.

Asking sentences end with a question mark.

Have I missed the train?

GRAMMAR *Focus*

Copy the sentences below into your book.
End each **telling sentence** with a full stop.
End each **asking sentence** with a
question mark.

1 What time is it

2 I am late for school

3 Did you eat your breakfast

4 What did you have

5 I had tea and toast

Look at this picture.

Remember the full stops and question marks.

1 Write three **telling sentences** about the picture.

2 Write three **asking sentences** about the picture.

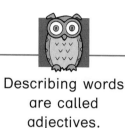

Describing words

Describing words tell us more about a person or a thing.

Describing words make sentences more interesting.

We can write about the picture like this:

The waves tossed the ship.

This is a more interesting sentence, using describing words:

The **huge** waves tossed the **battered** ship.

GRAMMAR *Focus*

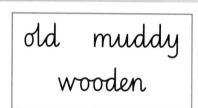
old   muddy   wooden

Choose a **describing word** from the box to make each sentence more interesting.
Write the sentences in your book.

1 The fire is burning the house.

2 The book is torn.

3 The man climbs out of the ditch.

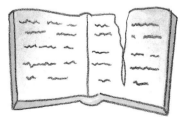

Use **describing words** of your own to make these sentences more interesting.

1 The balloon is in the sky.

2 The tiger lives in the jungle.

3 The old man has a stick.

4 The boy is making a tree house.

Check-up 3

The alphabet

Fill in the missing letters.

1 a b _ _ e f _ h i

2 j _ l _ n _ p _ _ _

3 S T _ V _ X _ _

Alphabetical order

Put the words in **alphabetical order**.

1 nut   man   owl

2 dig   bat   car

3 Lee   Hannah   Caroline

4 Ryan   Bob   Sita

Naming words

A Write the **naming words** from each of these sentences.

1 Put the cup on the table.

2 I have my book and pen.

3 Can you find the shoes?

B Write a sentence using each of these **naming words**.

1 snake   2 game   3 cart

4 tree   5 street   6 stamp

Describing words

A Write the **describing words** from these sentences.

1 This is a steep hill.

2 These are hard sums.

3 It is a dark night.

B Write a sentence using each of these **describing words**.

1 small   2 tall   3 fresh

4 best   5 dusty   6 flat

Doing words

A Write the **doing words** from these sentences.

1 Tony swims every day.

2 The girls ride their bicycles.

3 My cat sleeps in my bedroom.

B Write a sentence using each of these **doing words**.

1 walk   2 hunts   3 eat

4 shouts   5 write   6 runs

More than one

Make a list of the words that mean **more than one**.

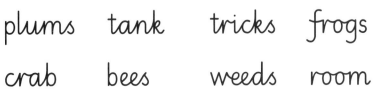

plums   tank   tricks   frogs

crab   bees   weeds   room

Special naming words

Write the **special naming words** with capital letters.

wave   greg   barn   george

card   mr little   peggy   bert

star   mrs pope   andy   farm

Sentences

A Copy these **sentences**.
   Add the **capital letters** and **full stops**.

1 he will go to a cricket match

2 there is no post today

3 here is the book you wanted

B Make **sentences** by putting the words in the right order.

1 has bicycle A wheels. two

2 book. reading am I good a

3 gone Dad shops. to has the

Questions

Which of these are **questions**?
Write the questions with question marks.

1 Is it raining

2 The weather is fine

3 Will I need an umbrella